Sing to Him,
sing His praise,
proclaim His wondrous deeds.
Glory in His holy name;
Rejoice O hearts
that seek the Lord!
1 Ch. 16:9-10

First Edition Printed in the U.S.A. by Concord Litho Co., Inc., Concord, New
Hampshire 03301-0464

The Symphony of Life

from the Salesian Collection

Compiled and Edited by
Sara Tarascio

Illustrated by
Paul Scully, Frank Massa and Russell Bushée

Contents

Birds He gave wings
To soar to the sky;
Man He gave thoughts
To attain heaven's heights.

Loise Pinkerton Fritz

God Made Them All!

There is a purpose in this world
    For every living thing -
For flowers and trees and animals,
    And birds upon the wing.

God made them all, the great and small,
    The mighty and the meek,
And we should treat them one and all
    With kindness when we speak.

For all that God created
    is precious in His sight
From the songbirds in the morning
    To the creatures of the night.

How dreary daily life would be
    Without these living things,
From the nuzzle of a kitten
    To an eagle's golden wings.

We must love them and protect them,
    And treat them with respect,
For surely we might lose them
    If we treat them with neglect.

Clay Harrison

... and God saw
all the things
that He had made,
and they were
very good.
Gen. 1:31

Morning in June

Oh, what is more joyful
than morning in June?
The air is sweet-scented
and songbirds in tune.
Morning glory trumpets
sip nature's cool dew
On gossamer spider webs,
dazzling to view.
The bountiful garden
awaits to bestow
Plump, fresh, crispy vegetables
row after row.
God's summer world's smiling
with June's special charms.
Go thankfully greet it
with welcoming arms!

Louise Pugh Corder

*Great and wonderful
are your works,
Lord God Almighty...*
Rev. 15:3

Humble Missions

For each of us, there is a reason
Why we live upon this earth -
Why the Lord has chose to bless us
With the sanctity of birth;
There's a purpose for our being
And a mission to fulfill
But we cannot know its nature
Or the Lord's Eternal will.

It is, seldom, deeds of greatness -
That He plans to have us do -
And we will not profit riches,
But for blessings that ensue;
They are simply humble missions
That will never bring us fame
But will justify our being
And do honor to His name.

Michael Dubina

Close to Thee

The Lord and I, we have our time
Of love, and talks, and prayers sublime,
These are special moments willed
When He takes charge, and I am stilled.
He's told me of all blessed things,
The summers, winters, falls and springs,
The graces that come unto you
About the earth and Heaven, too.
Some things are hard to understand
The differences of God, and man,
Though by His voice I hear no word,
'Tis within prayer that He is heard.
Together in our quiet way
I feel the joy of many things,
It seems I hear small voices pray
And feel the brush of Angels' wings.
Of course I feel this in my heart
'Tis when I pray, then God I find,
'Tis when our heart and soul are true
That God is close to me and you.

James Joseph Huesgen

God's Majesty
is Everywhere

The sky is blue as a robin's egg,
   the grass is emerald green.
God's majesty is everywhere -
   His glory daily seen.

Blossoms of peach, pear and plum,
   drift softly on the breeze,
And songbirds sing a joyful song
   from resurrected trees.

A fawn was seen upon the lawn,
   an eagle soars above.
Moonbeams sparkle dusk to dawn
   to fill the night with love.

From ocean floors to mountains high,
   to prairies in between,
God's majesty is everywhere -
   His glory daily seen.

         Clay Harrison

My Every-Hour God . . .

God of the morning, newborn day,
Sparkling and fresh and bright,
Grant me the wisdom to use it well,
Thank You for dawning's light.

God of the noonday, walk with me
Under fair skies above,
Help me to show in all that I do
Reflections of Your great love.

God of the twilight, peaceful hour,
End of a blessed day,
My heart in gratitude kneels to You,
Stay near me as I pray.

God of all hours, nighttime comes
Bringing me quiet rest,
Safe in the knowledge that by Your grace
I am forever blest.

Lee Simmons

In the Bible

In the bible you'll be finding
    Exactly what you need -
Answers to your questions,
    Advice that you should heed -

Faith that gives you wisdom
    To trust where trust should be,
And not believe that there is bad
    In ev'rything you see -

Hope that gives you courage
    To face another day
And feel that any sorrow
    Is never here to stay -

Love that changes all your thinking
    And makes you glad you trod
The pathway that was beautiful
    Because you walked with God.

Rachel Hartnett

*... rejoice O hearts
that seek the Lord.*
1 Ch. 16:10

Never Alone

He can calm the troubled waters
    When you walk in dark despair,
There is hope when you feel helpless
    Knowing that the Lord is there.

Sharing in your sunshine moments
    Or in valleys deep and wide,
He will never, ever leave you
    He is always by your side.

There's no other friend so faithful
    Through the sunshine and the rain,
Through the teardrops and the laughter
    In your joy and in your pain.

We could never ever thank Him
    For His love He gives so free,
Never changing . . . never ending
    Throughout all eternity.

Oh the wonder of all wonders
    As we live from day to day
Knowing that we have a Father
    Who is with us all the way.

Gertrude B. McClain

14

Inner Sanctuary

I have an inner sanctuary
    And friend, you have one too,
The Holy Spirit dwells inside
    The Bible says -- it's true.

Sometimes I stand beneath the stars
    In stillness of the night
And in my sanctuary there
    I marvel at His might.

His handiwork! -- He made it all,
    His glory it declares.
He's strong in pow'r -- not one star fails,
    They're Heaven's golden stairs.

Our earth is such a little thing
    Compared to galaxies
And I am less than nothing yet
    His Spirit dwells in me.

Within your sanctuary, friend,
    Does Jesus meet with you?
If not, I urge you to repent
    And His friendship renew.

        Luther Elvis Albright

His Love Abides

When friendships fail along life's way
And loneliness invades,
Friend, take your burden to the Lord...
His mercy never fades.
Your hurt and pain He understands;
He offers calming peace.
His loving touch will heal your wounds
And bid the teardrops cease.
And soon your heart will smile again
As He sets things aright,
For in His presence there is joy
And lonely hours take flight.
Oh blessed truth in which to trust
When life has lost its song...
Though friends forsake, His love abides,
Forever sure and strong!

Beverly J. Anderson

All God's Children

We're all God's children on this earth,
and individually
He is a Father to us all,
as only He can be.
He knows the yearnings of each heart,
over and above,
And none of us outgrow our need
For all His precious love.

We're all God's children on this earth,
However near or far,
Each face, each voice is dear to Him,
As different as we are.
He never loses track of us,
No matter where we go,
Nobody is an orphan
In God's family, you know.

We're all God's children on this earth,
The richest and the poor,
He loves each single one of us,
Of that we can be sure.
And when we say "Our Father
Up in Heaven," once again
The Lord bends down to listen,
And He softly says "Amen."

Grace E. Easley

As Summer Bids Farewell

Summer must have slipped away
I saw a leaf fall down,
In slowest kind of disarray
It softly touched the ground.

There seems to be a hint of gold
emblazoned here and there,
still on the tree a loveliness
of green still lingers fair.

As summer bids a fond farewell
In colors bright and bold,
excitement seems to fill the air
and beauty to behold.

And once again in majesty
of colors that are rare,
God holds the autumn in His hand
paints beauty everywhere.

Katherine Smith Matheney

Recognize God's Blessings!

God blesses us in many ways,
In different ways each day.

Some days He washes our hearts with tears
On others, the sun has its way!
A letter, a call, a bird's sweet song,
Or just being alive and part of the throng.

A chat with a friend, the payment of bills,
An endearing word that cures many ills!
The smile of a neighbor, a cheery hello
From someone you pass, whom you don't even know!

Completing a task begun long ago,
Or finding a recipe that you wanted so!
Finding a neighbor who needed you
To help with a task that was too hard to do.

To sit with a grandchild, to fix a bike,
To hear "I wuv you" from a little tyke!
To have God's blessing in some small way
Is to recognize it every day!

Rahya Montuori

Slow Me Down A While

Today, I'm in a hurry, Lord.
There's much I need to do.
Slow me down a while, that I,
Might share some time with You.

There are many who are lost, Dear Lord,
Who cannot find their way.
You know each sparrow, man, and child,
Embrace each one, I pray.

Many hurt and hunger, Lord,
I pray Thy Will be done.
Slow me down to give You praise,
For blessings, everyone.

As for me, Dear Lord, I cannot ask
For more than You have given.
Slow me down, that I may lift,
My grateful prayers to Heaven.

If any day, I fail to pray,
Lord, slow me down a while.
Let me reflect upon Your grace,
Before another mile.

Nancy W. Tant

20

A Dog Lover's Prayer

My prayer book's unconventional,
An album scarred with age.
The dogs who shared their lives with mine
Stand out on every page.

The spaniels of my childhood days,
All floppy ears and fluff;
The dobermans who shared my bed,
Magnificent and tough.

Though some folks picture Heaven's gates
Atop a golden stair,
The precious photos in my book
Inspire this humble prayer:

"Lord, lead me to a sun-washed field,
Then send them one by one;
Let yelps of joy lead wagging tails
As to my arms they run.

Sad eyes so pleading, paws that beg,
A symphony of barks,
Invite a romp in fragrant grass
To songs of meadowlarks.

This Heaven that I pray for, Lord,
Where lilacs scent the air,
Is blessed with all the dogs I've loved
Who come to greet me there."

Toni Fulco

The Lord's Bouquet

I picked a bouquet for Jesus
And put it in a vase;
Then I humbly bowed my head,
And said my dinner grace.

I lit a candle with a match,
And blessed the glowing flame
And thanked the Lord for daily bread,
And praised His holy name.

The vase that holds the Lord's bouquet
Is just a small pint jar;
Because I have no proper one
To thank the Morning Star.

Nevertheless I thank thee Lord,
For all I have today
Including the homey little jar
That holds the Lord's bouquet.

Evelyn Damron

The Dinner Guest . . .

Tonight I set the table;
It was a table set for two -
I used my finest linens,
And the silverware was new...

Tonight I set the table;
It was ladened with His food -
I served faith and hope and goodness,
And a dish of brotherhood...

Tonight I set the table
With a plate of peace and love;
Than I spread the cloth with kindness,
And sweet mercy from above...

Tonight I set the table,
And received a great reward,
For my guest arrived to bless it;
I was waiting for the Lord!

Hope C. Oberhelman

23

Autumn Splendor

As autumn flaunts its splendor
Of reds and golds and brown;
As the air turns kinda nippy,
And the leaves come tumbling down;
We know that God's been busy
Changing nature's dress.
'Tis the season to be thankful,
For we are truly blessed.

Lois N. Ayers

The Artist of Autumn

The Artist of Autumn is busy,
painting His canvases rare;
which those produced by mere mortals,
can never begin to compare;

For the hands of this masterful Craftsman,
give life to each stem and each sheaf;
and tints, with astounding perfection,
rich textures on each separate leaf.

He claims the world as His subject:
the deserts and valleys and hills;
nor do scenes of the farmlands and prairies
escape His breathtaking skills.

O He gives with His talents, unequalled,
a freshness and fragrance to air;
and garments of flame for the foliage,
but Autumn's are privileged to wear.

Therefore I always feel anxious
when this special season draws near;
for soon with His paintbox of magic,
will the Artist of Autumn appear.

Don Beckman

Give thanks to the Lord...
to Him who alone
does great wonders...
Ps. 136:3-4

God Stands By You

God stands by you to help you
When trouble comes your way.
He stands by you to help you
At any hour of day.

God stands by you to guide you
When you are in distress.
He stands by you to guide you
And bring you happiness.

God stands by you to lead you
And show you wrong from right.
He stands by you to lead you
And be your guiding light.

God stands by you most steadfast
Through sorrow and despair.
God stands by you awaiting
Your every call and prayer.

Harold F. Mohn

Beyond Ourselves

We sometimes miss a blessing
    that's right before our eyes
Preoccupied by earthly things
    which make us "wordly wise."

We fail to see beyond ourselves
    hearts that we have broken,
And we forget the angry words
    that we in haste have spoken.

We fill our lives with selfish things
    forgetting those in need,
And miss the joy that sharing brings
    in our effort to succeed.

How blessed we are when we believe,
    and praise God with our lips,
For when we reach beyond ourselves -
    we touch His fingertips!

Clay Harrison

27

Autumn's Magic

The air is crisp, wild geese fly high
And I view Autumn with a sigh;
The leaves are dancing to and fro
In rhythm with the winds that blow.

The shades of Autumn sport a blush
That's envied by the palette's brush,
And I stand spellbound by this treat
As twirling leaves entwine my feet.

The fruits of labor now reveal
Row upon row of ripened fields,
And through a distant Autumn haze
Friendly scarecrows gently wave.

The harvest moon's enchanting glow
Is prelude to the Winter's snow,
And I must gather memories
That I may recall days like these.

Catherine Janssen Irwin

God's Artistry

Lord, I stand in wonderment
As Your paintings I survey;
A palette of vibrant colors
On this warm, clear autumn day.

The trees are laden with leaves so bright
Of yellow, red and gold.
No human artist could ever paint
A tree so lovely to behold.

The fields are filled with golden grain.
Harvest time's at hand;
Orange pumpkins in the field,
Contentment o'er the land.

The setting sun sets sky on fire.
The harvest moon is bright.
The crisp night air portends Jack Frost
On this lovely autumn night.

So when I go to sleep at night,
Lord, I know that You are there,
Always watching over me,
To let me know You care.

Grace Lewis

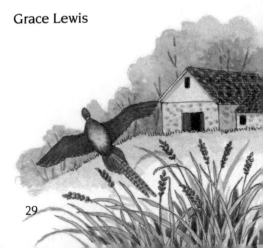

Mama's Empty Chair

When I was just a little boy -
    And mama was alive -
There was a special thing she did
    That taught me faith and pride:
She always set an extra place -
    At every festive fare -
And placed a lighted candle -
    Before an empty chair.

She said it was an honored place
    For loves that passed away
And for the Spirit of the Lord
    To share our festive day.
    So, now, I do - as mama did -
And pray that she will share
    Each place of honor that I set -
Before an empty chair.

Michael Dubina

Team Work

Please help me dear God
To write well today's page
For it's my life's story I'm writing
And I'm on the stage.

The things that I write
And the things that I say
May well help another
In some special way.

Help me Lord to listen
And answer wisely when asked
And work ever so willingly
And perform well each task.

Let me share joys of laughter
And love from my heart
To encourage another
And give him a start.

Let me rejoice in the splendor
And hear well Your voice
So that when my day is over
I'll give thanks and rejoice.

Rejoice that together
We wrote well a page
With You as Director
And me on the stage.

Chris Zambernard

*My help is
from the Lord
who made heaven
and earth.*
Ps. 121:2

My Father Speaks

"Open your heart," He said to me,
  "And taste the wind and taste the sea,
I've tossed the waves and stirred the air
  in freedom, with my perfect care.

I've scattered shells upon the sand,
  and driftwood, too, from forest-land,
And heaped the mountains closely by
  to catch the glow of evening sky.

I've made them all with you in mind
  and firmly left my prints behind,
That through my work your heart will see,
  I love you, child, stay close to me."

Maureen Dentler

Dawn in Summer

In summertime I like to rise
Before the dawn is here
And watch the darkness leave the sky
And slowly disappear.
All nature seems to stir itself
Without the slightest sound
Except the singing of the birds
Above the waking ground,
And then bright colors start to blend
Across the morning sky
Before the sun is visible
To any human eye.
That is the hour when I like
To meditate and dream
And contemplate the nobler side
Of life's unending stream,
To count my blessings on this earth
And thank my God again,
That such as I may share His world
With all my fellowmen.

James J. Metcalfe

Leave the Old Boat There

Everything says summer's over,
But leave the old boat there,
We like to be reminded of
Sailing the blue lake where
Dreams drift in clouds over our heads,
Water flowers flare,
It was a pretty sunshine summer,
Yes, leave the old boat there.

When winter comes and locks us in
We like the old boat there,
Snow sadness seems to go away,
The trees don't seem so bare,
While the white silence clings to earth,
She seems to breathe a prayer,
"Summer will come again, you'll see,"
Yes, leave the old boat there.

Marion Schoeberlein

Be as a Beacon

As the rays of the sun
light the hours of the day
Let the warmth of Your love
show others the way.
Be as a beacon
to those who are lost
In the turbulent anger
of a heart tempest-tossed,
For anger and hate
harm the one who recalls
The sins made against him,
and builds up high walls.
If mercy and love
play a role in each life,
Avoiding all discord
with freedom from strife,
Then peace, joy and hope
will enter the soul,
And God's gentle compassion
will make that life whole.

Dolores Karides

Walls of Brick and Stone

We cannot build gates high enough
 Or fences that will hold
When pain or sorrow comes our way
 And hearts are sad and cold.

There are no walls of brick or stone
 No wealth or power to gain
That can hold back or overcome
 Our days of loss and pain.

But we must not despair, give up
 Because we know so well
Our God is gracious... In His time
 And He can never fail.

He may not lift the shadows yet,
 His time is not as ours,
And yet we know the thorns of life
 With Him are fragrant flowers.

So when our walls come tumbling down
 And sorrow comes our way,
There is no need for walls of doubt
 Just kneel right down and pray.

    Gertrude B. McClain

Prayer for Today

Good morning Lord, I'm ready
To start a brand new day.
Keep me calm in spite of all
I'm bound to face today.
Seal my lips 'lest I should put
My foot into my mouth,
Give me the strength to do my job,
Though in the North or South.

Good morning, Lord, I'm back again,
I've had a good night's sleep,
Perhaps things might run smoother,
If You will help me keep
My temper and my senses,
Until the day is through.
Help me forget my troubles,
And concentrate on You.

Grace E. Easley

I Listen

I listen to the morning -
    every sound at break of day
To the birds that sing so sweetly -
    as the summer finds its way,
To the melody of nature -
    little creatures soft and dear
And it seems my heart finds beauty
    at each precious time of year.

I listen to the buzzing
    of the bee within the rose
And I'm sure I hear the laughter
    of the breeze in sweet repose,
It's a silent kind of music
    as I sense it all around
Tiny insects lend their singing
    as they scamper on the ground.

I listen to the night sounds
    as the dusk would settle in
Crickets chirping in the treetops,
    as the shadows now begin,

Oft I hear the noisy locust,
    when the autumn days are near
Yet my mind and soul are happy
    with each wondrous sound I hear.

Tis a magic kind of beauty -
    like a symphony of God
A part of earth and heaven,
    where the worthy then would trod,
A peacefulness I treasure
    as each morning then would start
And because I know of heaven -
    I listen with my heart.

              Garnett Ann Schultz

Praise to Thee, my Lord,
* for all Thy creatures.*
*   St. Francis of Assisi*

Autumn Days

I love this season of the year
When days are crisp and honey-clear;
When hillsides turn a russet brown
And Autumn sunlight shimmers down
Caressing gently, bushes, trees,
And flecks with gold the fallen leaves.

I love October's splendored days
When meadows glow with amber haze,
When pines and firs in emerald green
Bring lovely beauty to the scene,
And maple's vivid crimson blaze
Adorns the lanes and wooded ways.

When in the country asters grow
In white and purple, row on row;
And lazy sunflowers nod and sway
'Mid fields of clover and sweet hay;
While up above in azure sky
Swirled cotton candy clouds drift by.

I love this season of the year
When days are crisp and honey-clear.
When nature paints in bold array
October's colors bright and gay.
Joy fills my heart on days like these
When God smiles thru the flame-touched trees.

Beverly J. Anderson

'Tis the Time

'Tis the time, when we should thank Thee,
For Your blessings to each one.
'Tis the time, when we remember,
All the great things Thou hast done.

'Tis the time, we share our bounty
With our neighbors, friends, our kin,
'Tis the time, to reap the harvest
When the hay is gathered in.

'Tis the time, to give our offerings,
That another may rejoice,
'Tis the time of true thanksgiving
Tell it forth with joyful voice.

Lily S. Thomas

*Be thankful unto Him
and bless His name.*
Ps. 100:4

Words To Live By

There are words to live by,
That hang upon my wall,
Insuring strength, reviving hope,
Whatever may befall.
A source of inspiration,
Whenever skies are grey,
Written very long ago,
But just as true today.

There are words to live by,
Upon a yellowed page,
Underlined by someone
In a long forgotten age.
A guide post for the weary,
A refuge from all fear,
The simple phrase,
"Keep silent child,
. . . And know that I am here!"

Grace E. Easley

*Be still and
know that I
am God.*
Ps. 46:10

43

*Lord, let there be a gentle spring within my heart,
where those who need serenity and comforting
may find a cool, sweet plenitude.*

Showers of His Grace

Like unto a mountain stream,
Are showers of His grace,
That cooleth down the thirsty sod,
The trav'lers sun - parched face.

His dear grace oft' blankets us,
As covers keep us warm,
From hurtful barbs that can't get in
Through His encircling arms!

Things that were impossible
With God not at the helm,
Become with Him the probable,
And well within our realm!

Yes, that which was so hard before,
Without His gift of grace,
So oft' is easy when you give
To God His reigning place!

Lynn Fenimore Nuzzi

45

Sleep

When in the night I cannot sleep
And trouble crowds my mind
I long to close my eyes and rest
And leave the world behind.

I must be still and know that God
Will soothe my fretful brow,
No need to think of yesterday
But only of the now...

When God is close and holds my hand
Then sad thoughts go away
My troubles melt into the air
And darkness turns to day.

I settle close within His arms
My faith is strong and deep
Tomorrow's in His loving hands,
The night was made for sleep.

Mable Warburton

The Snowflake

The snowflake drifted down in feathery ease,
Wafted on its flight by northern breeze;
And dazzling white, it turns the o'ercast day
To brilliant light, as in reflector's ray.

Each tiny snowflake takes its little place,
In landscape covered o'er with shimmering face;
And branches humbly bend beneath its weight,
Each clothed in all the pureness of the flake.

And in its hour, the crescent moon looks down
Upon the peaceful winter's blanket, wound
Around the earth in gentle wraps of snow,
And giveth barren earth a heav'nly glow.

Ah, pureness of the snow, the gentle flake,
Giv'n of God, that from our folly wake,
And see that in the crystal fount that flows,
There's cleansing, pureness as the snow.

Charles G. Ramsey

... wash me and I shall be
whiter than snow.
Ps. 51:7

47

Keep Praying

It matters not how much we ask
When any prayer we speak
How many blessings for our friends
Or for ourselves we seek,
God does not mind how often or
How pleadingly we call,
Indeed He warmly welcomes our
Petitions, one and all.
But we must understand that by
His wisdom great forever,
Some prayers are answered very soon
Some later, and some never.
For He knows what is best for us
And all for whom we pray
And whether He should help us, more
Than we deserve today.
And so each time we beg of God
Some favor to fulfill,
Let us be patiently resigned
To His most holy will.

James J. Metcalfe

Simple Things

Don't miss the smallest rainbow
   which crowns that rainy day,
For like the daily sunset,
   it quickly fades away.

Hear the music of the sea
   upon the rocks below,
And listen to the nightingale
   when summer breezes blow.

Watch the turning of the leaves,
   and you can be my guest,
To watch the sermon of the trees
   when every heart is blest.

Come, catch some falling snowflakes
   beside a country lane
Where we can make a snowman
   with derby hat and cane.

Life's too short if you're too busy
   to do these simple things -
So don't overlook that rainbow
   and puppy dogs and swings!

Clay Harrison

Wintertime

Like a fairyland, such a lovely sight
With the sky so blue and the ground pure white,
A bit of frost on the window pane
Tells us it's wintertime again.

The sparkling warmth of the old log fire
The peace we find in a heart's desire,
The untold joy of a dream sublime
Because in our world it is wintertime.

Wintertime, when the wind blows cold
And the snow that falls brings delight untold,
The biting air that can chill you through
The thrill of home when your day is through.

The little stream that is frozen hard
The snowman perched in the neighbor's yard,
Laughter and smiles that are yours and mine
Only because it is wintertime.

Garnett Ann Schultz

The Beautiful Snow

The beautiful snow! The beautiful snow!
Covering all of the earth below;
Even the spots unlovely and drab
Adorned as a bride so daintily clad!
And the air all around so refreshingly clean
Reminds me of God and His wisdom supreme,
Wrapping His hills in a blanket at night
To give us a world in an etching of white!
And seeing His work it thrills me to know
That He washes a soul even whiter than snow.
And finding a life, once cheerless and bare,
He suddenly places His loveliness there;
Not transient, as snow is, but something to stay
Long after the snowdrifts have melted away.
Oh, I think of Him always whenever I see
The touch of His fingers on hilltop and tree,
Stooping so kindly His love to bestow,
Like a calm benediction, the beautiful snow!

Alice Hansche Mortenson

... Though your sins
be like scarlet,
they shall become
white as snow...
Isaiah 1:18

51

Snowflake Sign

Dark clouds press down; the sky grows gray.
A winter snowfall's on its way!
White fragile flakes drift through the air -
Each one of them, a jewel rare
That falls upon the earth with grace,
Paints on our world a fresh, new face.

Gaze up with wonder at the sky
And catch a snowflake gliding by.
To marvel at the crystal art
Its icy beauty warms the heart.
Each frosty flake's unique design
Becomes an awesome, reverent sign -
The God who can a mountain make,
Still cares about one small snowflake!

Louise Pugh Corder

Home and Family

It's a time of lonely journeys,
When we walk through life, alone -
Over roads that lead to nowhere
And no path that leads to home -
For we cannot share in pleasures
That we see and hear each day;
They belong to happy households
We just pass along our way.

Every longing that we suffer
Adds a sadness to our lot,
For the joys, we see around us,
Are the cravings in our heart,
But they are not meant for travelers -
Who will walk through life, alone -
They are blessings of Lord Jesus
On the family and home.

Michael Dubina

Winter's Art

Winter is a poet who,
  in quiet meditation,
    writes of mountains blanketed
    by white precipitation.

Winter is an artist, too,
  and softly draws the scene
    of stillness in a frozen pond
    against a silent screen.

Winter's a musician,
  and if we're listening,
    the grace-note of God's love is played
    which no one's voice can sing.

Frankie Davis Oviatt

Trust

"You're skating on thin ice,
You're due for a fall" -
These tried-and-true phrases,
I heard someone call.

My chin firmly set,
my nose in the air,
I chose not to listen,
forgot how to care.

The skaters whizzed by me,
the wind in their face,
blades gleaming bright
as they started to race.

I wanted to follow,
my feet felt like lead,
I couldn't keep up,
fell behind instead.

"Take hold of my hand,
give me your arm,
Rely on my love,
I'll keep you from harm."

So trust in the Lord
to be your true Guide,
Skate with the Lord
always at your side.

Janet Collins

*The Lord is good
and gives strength
in the day of trouble;
and He knows them
that trust in Him.*
Nahm. 1:7

That Church of Long Ago

When I hear the church bell ringing
In the little country church,
It is then my thoughts turn backward
And my heart is stirred, so stirred.
For I see again familiar scenes
And faces dear to me;
O, in that fleeting moment
It's there I long to be.

Then silenced is the ringing bell,
The present comes to fore;
I must press on for there's a time
When man can work no more.
But what a privilege it is
To have these memories flow,
Bringing back those bygone days
And that church of long ago.

Loise Pinkerton Fritz

When Troubles Assail You,
God Will Not Fail You

When life seems empty and there's no place to go,
When your heart is troubled and your spirits are low,
When friends seem few and nobody cares
There is always God to hear your prayers -
And whatever you're facing will seem much less
When you go to God and confide and confess,
For the burden that seems too heavy to bear
God lifts away on the wings of prayer -
And seen through God's eyes earthly troubles diminish
And we're given new strength to face and to finish
Life's daily tasks as they come along
If we pray for strength to keep us strong -
So go to Our Father when troubles assail you
For His grace is sufficient and He'll never fail you.

Helen Steiner Rice

Used with permission of
The Helen Steiner Rice Foundation
Cincinnati, OH 45202

Life is a Walking Memory

Life is a walking memory,
  A shadow of the past;
Some thought or deed or saying
  Is put in word at last.

Some memories are tragedies,
  And some bring bitter pain,
And some bear marks of heartache
  As they're written on the brain.

One always can look in the past
  And sit and stare and dream;
It takes a man with purpose
  To foil this subtle scheme.

Yes, there are memories in my past
  Which I had best forget
And fight the battle to the last,
  Unto the goal He's set.

Cease idle dreaming in my mind
  And let my soul fly on,
To greater, richer, heights sublime
  Which God has called upon.

Charles G. Ramsey

A Refugee in Thee

When hopes that are brightest
Like autumn have flown,
When hearts that we treasured
Have left us alone,
O, where from the sadness
Of grief should we flee,
If faith had no refuge,
Dear Savior, in Thee?

When dark are the storm clouds
Above us that roll,
And wild are the surges
That break o'er the soul,
O, where from the tempest
Of life should we flee,
If faith had no refuge,
Dear Savior, in Thee?

Though faith may be tested
And love may be tried,
How peaceful the haven
Where all may abide;
Whate'er with the tempter
Our conflict may be,
We still have a refuge,
Dear Savior, in Thee.

Fannie Crosby

*My help is from
the Lord who made
heaven and earth.*
Ps. 121:1

59

Keep Looking Up

Keep looking up! 'Tis a wonderful view,
Then look around for some work to do.
Put trust in Him the whole day through.
Stop, listen for His voice to you!

The upward look, to know His will;
The outward look, to do His will
The upward look, to Him Who sends;
The outward look, to tell lost men.

Keep looking up! 'Tis a wonderful view
To see that Jesus cares for you.
Look in His face for friendship true.
The love, He gives, is just for you.

Then look around for work to do
To friends and foes that look to you
For love and hope they long to find
In you, where dwells our Lord Divine.

Charles G. Ramsey

Set your affection on
things above,
not on things on
the earth.
Col. 3:2

God's Child

I've seen the Sea few times in life
'Til then my doubt was driven,
I have not seen my God at all
Yet - I know there is a Heaven.

I cannot see soft breezes blow
But I can feel them kiss my cheek,
I hear my God in many ways
Tho' - I have yet to hear Him Speak.

God shows Himself in ways to me
His Love He will impart
With such a heartfelt aura
Placed deep within my heart.

O' souls of you who fear Him not
Those of you who flee
Take time to look around - listen -
He'll say - "My Child, it's Me!"

James Joseph Huesgen

*... happy are these
thy servants who
stand before you
always and listen
to your wisdom.*
1 Kings 10:8

I Will

I will forgive all my hurts in every measure,
I will clear my mind of earthly treasure.
I will sow kindness and love,
I will seek the Lord's help from above.

I will make peace, instead of rebelling,
I will be charitable, my love o'er welling.
I will show no discontent,
I will give thanks to the Lord and repent.

I will pay compliments instead of derision,
I will pray for help to make the right decision.
I will give praise with the right intent,
I will promise the Lord not to invent.

I will accept adversities coming my way,
I will be happy with the Lord's rate of pay.
I will put out my hand to anyone in need,
I will seek the Lord's help to do a good deed.

I will do my best to drive out sadness,
I will replace it with gladness.
I will strive to eliminate sorrow,
I will do it today, not tomorrow.

I will pray to the Lord to strengthen my intent,
I will accept His love and be content.

John J. Gruenenwald

Life

A portion of living
A portion of care,
A hope for the future
A dream we can share,
It's knowing and doing
The ups and the downs,
The moments we treasure
The smiles and the frowns.

Success we accomplish
The failures that come,
The clouds that may gather
The bright shining sun,
Each blessing God sends us
The heartaches and trials,
Pursuing tomorrow
Midst tears or midst smiles.

Tis all part of living
The give and the take,
The gains and the losses
The choices we make,
Accepting God's promise
Midst good times or strife
A portion of dreaming
The meaning of life.

Garnett Ann Schultz

I ask O Lord some purpose in my life;
help me to choose, while now I live,
something to keep before me as a goal.

A Place For Me

There is a special place in life,
That needs my humble skill,
A certain job I'm meant to do,
Nobody else can fill.
The hours are demanding,
And the pay is not too good,
And yet I wouldn't change it
For a moment, if I could.

There is a special place in life,
A goal I must attain,
A dream that I must follow,
For I won't be back again.
There is a mark that I must leave,
However small it be,
A legacy of love for those
Who follow after me.

There is a special place in life
That only I may share,
A little path that bears my name,
Awaiting me somewhere.
There is a hand that I must hold,
A word that I must say,
A smile that I must give, for there
Are tears to blot away.

There is a special place in life
That I was meant to fill,
A sunny spot where flowers grow
Upon a windy hill.
There's always a tomorrow,
And the best is yet to be,
And somewhere in this world I know
There is a place for me!

Grace E. Easley

*E*ach drop of water
flowing under the bridge
is a minute of life gone by,
and you cannot stop
its rushing flow
no matter how hard you try;
each flower that wilts
beside the stream
is another day that is gone forever,
so whatever you do
with this precious day,
it must be done now, or never.

Virginia Luers

... the source of
wisdom is a
flowing brook.
Prov. 18:4

A Summer's Day

A summer day is wondrous,
As sunshine kisses earth,
One feels a special pleasure
And bubbles o'er with mirth.

The sky is blue as azure,
The breezes soft and rare,
It makes one gay and happy
Child-like without a care.

The birds sing in the tree-tops,
Green fields and shrubs abound,
And little croaks and murmurs
Blend into summer's sound.

The far-flung country meadows
Wear daisies in their hair,
Farmlands look like patchwork quilts,
The views are warm and fair.

And in the eves at twilight,
The horizon turns to gold,
Then the wonders of the summer
Are so precious to behold.

Virginia Borman Grimmer

Only
A
Sparrow

If I were only a bird all day
And flew the whole day long,
Filled the air where'er I may
With my pretentious song,

How sweet t'would be to sit a bough
High up in the air
Surveying all beneath me
With just a sparrow's care.

I could jump the continents
Just like the storied bee,
Make all of the world and nature too
So, all-aware of Thee.

James Joseph Huesgen

My Garden

My garden is a magic place,
When cares of life hit hard,
There's healing for the mind and heart,
Working with the sod.
You plant a seed of hope,
Set trust plants in a row,
And Mother Nature does her part,
To make them grow - and grow.
The names of course are different.
But hope springs up anew,
With the seeds you plant or the plants you set
Trust returns to you.
Yes, when the cares of life are hard,
And my mind is all at Sea,
My garden is a sanctuary,
Between my God and me.

Lea Helms Davis

The Wishing Well

I wished for blue skies
They turned out grey,
I yearned for tomorrow
While it was still "today,"
I wanted dozens of friends
Who were all tried and true
I looked far and wide
But found only a few.

I dreamed of a future
Where riches abound,
And searched with a vengeance
But "nothing" I found.
To reach success
Was my Life's main goal
But I climbed the ladder
Without my Soul.

Life seemed a failure
All my dreams were shattered,
Then I met You Lord
And nothing else mattered.
Do wishes come true?
Who really can tell?
Yet I found Life and Hope
At my Wishing Well.

Eleanor Larson

The Lord Is My Shepherd

The Lord is my Shepherd,
And I am His lamb,
Who loves me in spite
Of the way that I am.
Who sees something in me,
That other folks miss,
And I sometimes think maybe,
Because of this
I've never felt bitter,
Unloved or alone,
Though sometimes I grieve for
My loved ones now gone.
For I've always believed in
The words He has said,
That the spirit lives on,
Though the body be dead.
And I feel closer to Him,
Because of His care,
And I know when I call Him,
That He will be there.
So I fear not the shadows,
So dark and so dim,
For my Shepherd will carry me
Safely through them.

Grace E. Easley

The Lord is
my shepherd,
I shall not want.
Ps. 23:1

71

God's Garden

Around about my garden,
In a very special place
Among the leaves and branches
And flowers shaped like lace,
I've found a special place to pray,
To start and finish every day.
The blooms, the thorns, the tangled vines
They all depict my life and times.
The joys, the pains, the webs I weave,
I lay them down, my cares I leave.

Around about God's garden
This world, His special place.
Among the strife and problems,
He protects me with His grace.
He smiles at my blooming,
Rains tears upon my pain.
He tends and bends to care for me,
Encourages my gain.
As I view life from God's garden,
Life is easier to see.
Amid His sacred garden
I can trace God's plan for me.

Katie Barrows

Providential Mercies

If God can take an earthen root
And grow a peony;
And plant within an acorn
The burstings of a tree;
If God can gown a little bird
And fill its heart with song -
Then He can take my feeble self
And make me sweet and strong.

If God can take a tiny seed
And nurture it to worth;
Dress the field and bushes
With flower-scented birth;
If He can govern suns and rains
And use them for our good -
I'm thus assured God works for me
In just the way He should.

There's not a sparrow drops its wing,
Not a human cry that falls,
But what God responds with all His love -
He hears our bleating calls!

Roxie Lusk Smith

73

Resource of the Flowers

I marvel at the wardrobe
  the fresh Spring flowers wear
    that serve as bright expressions
    of our God's abiding care.

The source behind their garments,
  so prim and proudly worn,
    is their unfailing confidence
      He'll see them thus adorned.

If He so clothes the flowers
  in such rich becoming hue,
    be sure He'll do the same for us,
    if we allow Him to.

But first we must be trustful
  His design for us is best;
    take root in that assurance;
    and let Him do the rest.

And if we blend our Will with His,
  the way the flowers do,
    we'll find our countenance and soul
    both glowingly renewed.

Don Beckman

*Consider the lilies
how they grow...
Solomon in all his glory
was not arrayed like
one of these.*
Luke 12:27

74

Light Your World

Let the light of God shine through
    as you go about your days.
In all the little things you do,
    try to do them in God's way.

You'll never know the happiness
    that a friendly smile can bring
to someone who's been feeling down -
    left out of everything.

The hurting heart will suddenly
    flip flop, and beat anew -
restoring hope and contentment
    all because of you!

A few flowers from your garden,
    some cookies, or some bread,
will show you care, and ease the pain
    of someone's aching head.

It's giving of yourself that counts
    in all things great and small -
to do His bidding, our very best,
    each time we hear Him call.

Our privilege is to serve our Lord,
    and spread His light on earth.
While we are stewards of His world,
    He judges our true worth.

Mary B. Conn

My Cabin of Dreams

It stands on a hill, my Cabin of Dreams,
And touches each lure of the sky -
And all that is fine of boulder and vine,
No log and no stone will deny.
It's simple and humble - each window is small -
Its roof is the bark of a tree,
But never a castle has ever been built
Whose dreams are more fonder to me.

There is not a gate where strangers must wait
For judgement of mission or aim;
The path to its door no step will deplore -
All strangers are welcomed the same.
Its timbers are rustic; its rafters are bold;
It tells of the meadow and mire,
But Heaven can only compare to the dreams
That live by the glow of its fire.

Yet all of this bounty I cannot divide
With friends whom I dearly adore;
And all of the riches God gave to my hearth
I cannot bequeath from its store.
A vestige of Heaven each friend may enjoy -
Each comfort and pleasure is free -
But I am the builder and dreamer of dreams
God gave to my cabin and me.

Michael Dubina

Dandelions

Dandelions in the grass,
On a bright spring day,
Brown bees buzz, and robins chirp,
Children shout and play.

Dandelion face up-turned
Like a yellow brush.
Short stemmed floweret adorns,
Green grass, deep and lush.

Dandelions pluckt in haste,
By little fingers,
Of the summer days to come,
Cheerful harbingers.

Soon each yellow face will wilt,
And the blossom fade,
Other flowers take their place
In the forest glade.

To keep our faces bright, and
Bravely live each day,
Is the lesson we can learn
From this flower gay.

Lily S. Thomas

The flowers appear
on the earth.
Song of Solomon 2:12

Never lose an opportunity of
seeing anything that is
beautiful; for beauty is
God's handwriting –
Ralph Waldo Emerson

Everywhere I Look

Everywhere I look I find
   Some wondrous handiwork of Thine,
Every single day I see
   Some lovely thing You've given me.
My heart almost overflows,
   At the sight of velvet rose,
Lacy fern, and birds that sing,
   Lord, You give me everything.

As the early morning breeze
   Softly stirs through leafy trees,
Comes the dawn all steeped in gold,
   More than my two arms can hold.
Silver stars throughout the night,
   Purple shadows, pale moonlight,
Turn my thoughts again to Thee,
   Lord, I fear You're spoiling me.

Everywhere I look I find
   Beauty of the richest kind,
Little joys throughout the day,
   Almost take my breath away.
How very precious I must be,
   That You should have such love for me,
And in each cranny, smallest nook,
   I find You, everywhere I look.

Grace E. Easley

God Is Not Dead

Alone, despondent and forlorn
I found myself one day,
My heart and mind could find no peace
Along life's troubled way.
The hopes and dreams that I possessed
Seemed shattered and in vain,
I felt that life was cruel and full
Of heartaches and great pain.
Then suddenly I heard a voice
Speak plainly in my ear,
"Have faith my friend, do not despair
For I am always near."
I felt a surge of strength within,
In some mysterious way,
And deep inside I know 'twas God
Who spoke to me that day.

Harold F. Mohn

Gather Round the Table

Gather round the table,
Share a laugh or two,
Say a prayer of blessing,
See a dream come true.

Gather round the table,
When the holidays are here,
The family comes together
To spread a little cheer.

Gather round the table,
Each place is set you see,
It's waiting for a loved one,
I know there's one for me.

We gather round the table,
Each night when day is through,
To thank the Lord for families,
And pray that you do too.

Nancy M. Smith

*Where two or three
are gathered in my
name, there am I
in their midst .*
Matt: 18:20

A House on the Shore

Let me live in a house on an ocean shore
Where the surf and sand do meet
Let me sit, my dear Lord, at the water's edge
Where the waves gently wash my feet.

Let me feel the sun's warmth, as it shines on my face,
Watch the sea gulls flying on high
Let me see the sun set, far out in the west,
Where the water seems to meet the sky.

But if, my dear Lord, plans that You have for me
Are not plans that I'm dreaming of,
Then Thy will be done, I'll be happy to know
I'm forever more bathed in Your love.

Albert N. Theel

Blessings

Inside our sunny kitchen,
Upon the window sill,
Are clay pots, full of flowers
Safeguarded from the chill.
Beside the curtained window
Is a favorite rocking chair,
Some books, a sewing basket,
For relaxing there.
A bright enameled kettle
Invites us to have tea,
When it starts to whistle
Loud and merrily.
When supper's on the table
And the grace is said,
We thank the Lord for blessings
And for our daily bread.

Elsie Natalie Brady

*And all these blessings
shall come upon thee
if you hear the voice
of the Lord, your God.*
Deut. 28:2

The Birds - The Flowers - A Sunny Sky

It's just a little lane quite hidden
By the bushes and the trees,
But you'll know it when you get there
By the birds' sweet melodies.

Although it may seem rough and bumpy
It's the grandest place to go,
For in the spring it's decked with violets
In the wintertime there's snow.

It's so quiet and so peaceful
In this little country lane,
But I know if once you go there
You are bound to go again.

For it's one of life's few pleasures
That is absolutely free,
The birds, the flowers, a sunny sky
Will welcome you with glee.

It's the closest thing to heaven
It's a joy you mustn't miss,
For it's more than just a country lane
It's the road to happiness.

Garnett Ann Schultz

84

He Called Me By Name

"He called me by name"
From the time of my birth,
Before I had met Him,
And valued His worth.
And because He was God,
He was able to see
That I had to have someone
To watch over me.

So He picked out an angel,
My own special one,
To guide and protect me,
'Til living was done.
Who had but one job,
And that was to be
A loving and loyal
Companion to me.

"He called me by name"
And the love in His eyes,
Promised me all
That this cold world denies.
A home with Him always,
In Heaven above,
Safe in the Kingdom
Of God's endless love.

Grace E. Easley

*I will give you treasures out of
the darkness and hidden riches
that you may know that I am
the Lord, the God of Israel,
who calls you by name.*
Isaiah 45:3

85

A Home

A home is more than plaster and paint
    Nice fancy trim and pretty or quaint.
A home is love and it breaths alive
    A heart that is warm and free inside.
It's a refuge each day of the year
    A blessing for all who hold it dear.
The size doesn't matter nor material inside,
    It's the feeling of peace where you abide
In serenity and God's loving care,
    Knowing each member is truly happy there.
Home is where we return at the end of the day
    To love one another so cares slip away.
When a home is built on humility and love
    God surely sends His blessings, from up above.
May your home be blessed, and may it ever be
    Your own special corner of eternity.

Edna Louise Gilbert

All is Well

The virgin white of winter
    Now wears a shawl of green
For all the trees are budding
    And flowers can be seen.

The snow that chilled us yesterday
    Has melted like a dream
For now the stone is rolled away
    Beneath the sunlight's gleam.

How sweet the sound of singing
    As songbirds now return,
And here below the rainbow
    Earth makes another turn.

For spring's a noble season,
    One of show and tell,
When God reveals His majesty
    And shows us all is well.

Clay Harrison

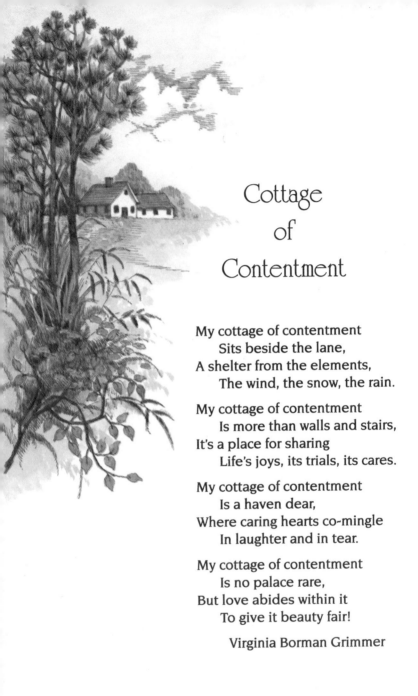

Cottage
of
Contentment

My cottage of contentment
　　Sits beside the lane,
A shelter from the elements,
　　The wind, the snow, the rain.

My cottage of contentment
　　Is more than walls and stairs,
It's a place for sharing
　　Life's joys, its trials, its cares.

My cottage of contentment
　　Is a haven dear,
Where caring hearts co-mingle
　　In laughter and in tear.

My cottage of contentment
　　Is no palace rare,
But love abides within it
　　To give it beauty fair!

Virginia Borman Grimmer

Formula

A cheerful smile when things go wrong,
meeting tears with joyful song;
patience when we'd rather run
than face a trial that's just begun,
progressing upward though the will
is tired, and wanting to stand still;

Silence when we would explode
and speak the bitterness... unload!
Give answers soft for cruel blow,
if we desire in grace to grow;
bravery when our hearts are faint,
this is required to be His saint!

Anna Lee Edwards McAlpin

*Order my steps in Thy word:
and let not any iniquity have
dominion over me.*
Ps. 119:133

Country Artist

If I could be an artist, I would paint
The sky at sunset's end, bright tangerine,
Which melts to saffron, then to mottled blue,
With whispers of deep mauve tucked in between.

I'd paint a barn, once red, now weathered gray;
A leaning fence; a tractor gone to rust;
A row of combines waiting in the field;
A country road by brambles caked with dust.

Then twilight would descend majestically
To set this treasured countryside aglow
With August's harvest moon beyond the hills
Where fields of wheat, like burnished copper, grow.

Oh, would that palettes swirled with dabs of rhyme,
And pens that flow with lilting poetry
Could match the great Creator in the sky,
Unequaled in His country artistry.

Sandra R. Lytle

In Every Heart

By acts of faith and deeds of love
And kindnesses of mind,
God's Kingdom - and its world of joys -
Is in our hearts, to find,
For - in each heart - He planted seeds
To nourish, from within,
That open up His World of Grace
To let us enter in.

For every need of life and love,
He gave us seeds to sow
And willed - to us - the right to choose
Which seeds we want to grow
So, we must sow and grow the seeds
That Christian loves impart
And He will light - within us all -
The kingdom in each heart.

Michael Dubina

Garden in My Heart

I have a garden in my heart
Where friendly flowers grow,
And each one has the gentle name
Of somebody I know.
Their petals are the memories
Of passing smiles and tears,
Their stems are sturdy shafts of love
That last throughout the years.
I tend my garden carefully
And keep its beauty bright,
Beneath a kindly sun by day
And faithful stars at night.
The wind may blow, the snow may fall
The rain may gather gloom,
But in the garden of my heart
The flowers always bloom.
I do not ever pluck them for
The vases on my shelves,
Because I know they would not last
Or multiply themselves.

James J. Metcalfe

A Simple Prayer

Lord help me to live
That others may
Be glad I chanced
To pass their way.
Help me to smile
Through worry and care,
Teach me that burdens
Lighten through prayer.

May it never be said
That I failed to lend
A helping hand
To the need of a friend.
Grant that seeing Christ
In others
I may recognize them
As my brothers.

Most of all let me live
In Thy grace
Content with my role
In the human race,
That when this earthly life
is through
I may share eternity
With You.

Eleanor Larson

The measure
of love
is to love
without
measure.
St. Francis de Sales

Life's Symphony

Oh, time the moments of my days,
Dear Lord, in perfect rhythm;
Not measured by an earthly score,
But harmonized in Heaven.
Oh, let me fix my eyes on Thee
So I will understand
The meaning of Thy slightest nod,
Each gesture of Thy hand.
And may I hear each whispered thought
So I will ever be
In readiness to play the part
That You have given me.

Forgive the times I've questioned this,
My small and humble score;
So oft ignoring 'holds' and 'rests,'
Alone I tried to soar
In swift allegro time and rushed
To carry out Thy will,
When suddenly the music stopped,
I heard Thy voice "Be still."
Had I been watching carefully,
Dear Lord, I would have known
That no one plays sweet music in
Life's symphony alone.

Alice Hansche Mortenson

Beside the Sea

In happiness I reign supreme,
Under the spell of the sea;
I hear the ocean's mighty roar
Singing her songs to me.

Waves caress the sandy shore
On a seaside holiday,
Salt sprayed breezes kiss my cheek,
Sea gulls romp and play.

I lingered lost in reverie
By my mystical, magical sea,
A perfect day that will remain
Locked in my memory.

Golden sunbeams warm my soul,
Shimmering everywhere;
Then suddenly I felt the touch
Of God's presence there.

Nora M. Bozeman

Sandcastles

I learned a needed lesson
At the shore one summer day
As I watched the little children
Building sandcastles at their play.
It is wise to build for heaven
For life's tides ebb and flow,
Earth's treasures are not lasting
We must one day let them go.
But the good deeds of the blessed
To the needy of the earth
Will please our Heavenly Father
And have eternal worth.

Sister Mary Gemma Brunke

97

September Abundance

As summer turns to autumn
Throughout September land,
Rich, ripened harvest plenty
Abounds at every hand.

The earth is full of fragrance
Of mellow fruit and hay.
The sky's an azure canvas,
And crickets chirp all day.

Vermillion leaves are scattered
Among remaining green.
Wild goldenrod and asters
Enhance the roadside scene.

I feel a reverent wonder
At such abundant love
Sent from a gracious Father
Sustaining from above.

Louise Pugh Corder

September Moods

As Autumn shadows lengthen,
And shorter grow the days
I know I love September
In so many different ways!
September rolls up all the moods
That other months have given
And sends them flying on a cloud,
Straight to seventh heaven!
The wistful moods of rainy days
Seem to echo in the fun
Of happy hours remembered,
Or beach and wind and sun!
The moods I felt in early Spring
Beside a crackling fire
Seem to renew, in Autumn's dream,
Some unfulfilled desire!
The wintry winds spoiled many a plan,
Dipping the mood quite low,
But the sparkling sun on the crisp,white snow
Made me want to go, go, go!
September spurs the memories
Of the months as they came and went
And stirs one to evaluate
Just how the time was spent!
The Fall is frosting on life's cake
The moods, the savory spice,
But September is the cake itself,
Because it is so nice!

Rahya Montuori

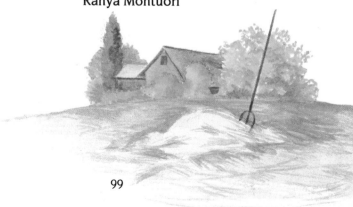

The Fruits of

Peace

With love plant seeds of peace today;
Tend them in a careful way,
Anger, greed and rancor thrive
Where discontent lets them survive.

Weed the garden of your heart;
Give the peaceful plants a start.
Nourish them with constant prayer;
Flowers of strength will blossom there.

Storms of life may beat and bruise them;
God will use the storms to prove them,
Harvest time will show increase:
Goodness, joy - the fruits of peace.

Ethel H. Kleppinger

Peacemakers who sow in peace
raise a harvest of righteousness.
James 3:18

Prayers Can't Be Answered
Unless They Are Prayed

Life without purpose is barren indeed -
There can't be a harvest unless you plant seed,
There can't be attainment unless there's a goal,
And man's but a robot unless there's a soul...
If we send no ships out, no ships will come in,
And unless there's a contest, nobody can win...
For games can't be won unless they are played,
And prayers can't be answered unless they are prayed...
So whatever is wrong with your life today,
You'll find a solution if you kneel down and pray
Not just for pleasure, enjoyment and health,
Not just for honors and prestige and wealth...
But pray for a purpose to make life worth living,
And pray for the joy of unselfish giving,
For great is your gladness and rich and your reward
When you make your life's purpose the choice of the Lord.

Helen Steiner Rice

Used with permission of
The Helen Steiner Rice Foundation
Cincinnati, OH 45202

Today

Today I promise I'll be true
And do the things I ought to do.
I'll keep my thoughts all shining bright
My spirits buoyant, clean and light.

I'll speak with calm and careful tongue
Rejoice when I see work well done.
I'll love my neighbor down the street
And guard my sometimes wayward feet.

I'll seek the best, the fine and true,
And let no angry thoughts come through.
I'll offer help when need I see,
For that's the way I ought to be.

And can I, Lord, this promise keep,
And when at night lay down to sleep
Remember that my thanks are due
To God, the One who saw me through.

Mabel Warburton

Life's Treasures

There are no treasures I possess
That bring eternal happiness.
I covet not the things of gold
That some desire to have and hold.
I have no diamonds, pearls and such
That others tend to love too much,
For these are temporary things
To which the Christian never clings.
Better far are the things of God,
The golden grain and bursting pod...
Peace of mind, a contented heart,
A faith that sets our lives apart.
I treasure more my daily bread
Than souvenirs of the ancient dead.
I'd rather have a loving friend,
A wife on whom I can depend.
These are the treasures I possess
That fill my life with happiness.

Clay Harrison

A man's life consisteth not in the
abundance of the things
which he possesseth.
Luke 12:15

The Power of Faith

Each cross that you may have to bear,
Each fear that brings duress,
Will never be too great for you
If God's love you possess.

When pain and sorrow are your lot
And drive you to despair,
You will find hope and sustenance
If you seek God in prayer.

When goals in life seem out of sight
And efforts are in vain,
Have faith and with God's helping hand
Each one you can attain.

No power on earth is greater
Than faith that you possess.
It will transcend all other things
And bring true happiness.

Harold F. Mohn

Seek And Ye Shall Find

On a stroll one sunny morning
I set out to gather jewels
I left behind all doubt and worry
But took along essential tools.

Tools of wisdom, faith, and patience
And a basket full of dreams
To be filled to overflowing
From the priceless gift of Him.

I also took along the positive
And 'twasn't long until I found
A humming voice so clear and chiming
Though there was no one around.

I also felt a sweet caressing
As the warm wind softly draped
E'er so gently 'round about me
And I knew it was God sent.

The stroll continued as I gathered
All the jewels that I could hold
I then compared them to His riches
Of a flawless... "Gift of Gold"...

Chris Zambernard

Take Time To Pray

Do you have a lot of problems
That you just can't set aright,
That seem to follow you each day
And awaken you at night?

Do you feel your spirit slipping
With so many faded dreams,
As you try to put together
Life that's splitting at the seams?

Perhaps you've got to learn to give
Before your right to take,
The branch that bends not in the wind,
It will most surely break.

Just ask the Lord to help you,
He'll guide you each new day,
You'll find your burdens lifted
If you take the time to pray.

Albert N. Theel

Test of Faith

My heart is very heavy
   With the burdens of this day
For it has been a time of trials -
   Of struggle and dismay -
And all my prayers have been in vain
   To comfort my despair
Or bring me blessings of my Lord
   For faith in holy prayer.

Yet, I am not disposed to cry
   For all in disarray
For God, I'm sure, has made this day
   For me to find my way
And means, for me, to walk alone -
   To prove my faith is strong -
When prayers are empty of reward
   And everything goes wrong.

Michael Dubina

Majestic Steeple

I see you from the wooded path
I see you from the hill
I see your shadow gently fall
Upon my window sill.

When skies are warm and sunny
Or cold with rain or snow
You loom tall and inspiring
And protect me here below.

Your cross glows in the sunset
A reverence I do feel
And thankful prayers come to my lips
As chiming bells do peal.

Majestic steeple in the sky
I see you everywhere
You bring me comfort and contentment
For I know that God lives there.

Grace P. Quattrone

The Wayside Chapel

There's a little wayside chapel
Where the fragrant wildflowers grow,
And it's here I go to worship
The Lord God Whom I know.
He is the great Creator,
To earth He holds the deed;
He is the loving Shepherd
Who watches over me.

In this little wayside chapel
There's a reverence that glows,
For where two or three are gathered
In His name, He's there, I know.
So when darkness veils the sunlight
And the heart is sorely pressed,
In this little wayside chapel,
Here God grants me peace and rest.

Loise Pinkerton Fritz

*For where two or three are
gathered together in my name,
there am I in the midst of them.*
Matthew 18:20

Pets

You've given many gifts, oh Lord,
That brighten, help and cheer,
Like butterflies and sunset skies,
But of gifts there's none more dear
Than pets, dear dogs and cats and all
Who share our smiles and cares
And wag a friendly tail or purr,
Or look with ever caring eyes
Into our own, as though they were
Studying each thought we have,
And when their short, good lives
Are done and they have gone away,
They leave a sorrow. Yes, but too,
A joy that still does stay
On through the years ahead,
And brings a tear but most a smile,
For what they shared with you and me
Helped make our lives worthwhile.

Minnie Boyd Popish

110

My Special Time

There's a time that is so special:
When the day is fresh and new -
Sitting out upon my front porch,
While the ground is laced with dew.

With a mug of fresh-made coffee,
And my kitten by my side,
All my worries take a back seat;
All my problems have to slide.

For it's my own time to marvel
At the handiwork of God,
As the soft breeze sifts the treetops,
And the flowers give a nod.

Birds unite to sing a chorus;
They're so happy to be free.
Squirrels are playing on the front lawn;
Such a lovely sight to see.

All the grass looks somehow greener,
And the sky's of bluest hue,
As I view them from my front porch -
When the day is fresh and new.

Diana Sue Lindley

Speak To Me Lord Jesus

Oh speak to me Lord Jesus
I long to hear Your voice
Banishing my sorrows,
Bidding my sad heart rejoice.

You know I'm oft so busy
Rushing here and there,
That I do most the talking
When I kneel down in prayer.

Seem so much to ask for
So much to tell You too,
I rarely stop to listen
Yet I need to hear from You.

So now I will be quiet
Hushed my mind and heart,
Speak Lord in the stillness
Your word to me impart.

Speak to me and show me
What You would have me do,
Then give to me the courage
To go and work for You.

Rosemary J. Tivey

Speak, Lord;
for thy servant heareth.
1 Samuel 3:9

112

My
Morning Prayer

Help me be the smile
One someone's face and not the frown.
Help me be the one who picks them up
Not puts them down.

Help me be the rose
In someone's life and not the thorn.
Help me be the rainbow in their sky
And not their storm.

Help me warm a heart
Not be the one who brings the snow.
Help me be the dew when they need it, Lord
to grow.

Help me be the light
Not be the one who turns them out.
Help me instill confidence
Not misery and doubt.

When day is done
Let there be one
Who holds a memory

Of love and joy
To know that they
Are loved, by Thee... and me.

Debbie Immel North

Thou hast given so much to me,
give one thing more...
a grateful heart; not thankful
when it pleaseth me...
but such a heart whose pulse
may be Thy praise.
George Herbert

The Little Bird

I walked the hills this morning.
My heart felt sad in me.
I heard a small bird singing
The sweetest melody.

It seemed to come from everywhere
I hunted high and low.
But where God's singer hid himself
Was not for me to know.

I thanked Him for the little bird
I thanked Him for the song
I thanked Him for the message heard
And then the bird was gone.

I know that my God loves me
He sent that bird you see,
To put a song within my heart
And set my spirit free.

Nancy M. Smith

... we were rescued
like a bird from
the fowler's snare...
Ps. 124:7

115

The Chapel On The Hill

As twilight shadows softly fall
I slowly wend my way,
To the little Chapel on the hill
To meditate and pray.

The weary burdens of this world
At last are all forgot,
My steps are quickened as I near
The Holy place of God.

The organ's softly playing
As I step inside the door,
And a quiet contentment fills me
That I never knew before.

Then I bow my head in silence
And I lift my heart in prayer,
And unburden all my troubles
To the only One who cares.

And as I pray, I seem to hear
Him answer me and say,
"Thy sins are all forgiven, son,
Go forth and mend thy ways."

Now, as I leave that Hallowed ground
And slowly homeward plod,
My heart is filled with solace
From Communion with my God.

Catherine MacDonald

God's Children

Although God loves the whole wide world
    And blesses every part,
I think He has a special place
    For children in His heart.

I think He cherishes their smiles,
    Their eagerness and mirth,
And their appreciation of
    The wonders of His earth.

I think He listens closely to
    Whatever words they say;
I think He follows them to school
    And watches them at play.

And when they go to bed at night,
    He probably is there,
To see that they have happy dreams
    Beneath their tousled hair.

All children in a special way
    Belong to God above,
And I am sure He favors them
    With everlasting love.

        James J. Metcalfe

Treasures Along the Way

How oft, among the waving fields
    of life, so fair and wide;
We, careless, take the husk and straw
    And cast the grain aside.
And on its pleasant, gravelly strand,
    With jewels richly strown;
We pick the pebbles and the shells
    And leave the gems alone.

And in the hall, and at the mart,
    And on the land-street fair;
We choose the worse, and fail to see
    The wondrous treasures there.
The treasure of the kindly deed,
    The gem of vital thought,
The riches of the glorious scene
    The hand of God hath wrought.

There's treasure on the broad highway,
    There's treasure in the street,
There's treasure in the looks and smiles
    Of those we chance to meet;
There's treasure in the friendly voice,
    The song and e'en the laugh;
Then make it yours and throw aside
    The worthless stones and chaff.

Bruce E. Hoad, Sr.

There's No Limit To God's Love

In the lake I see reflected
    The moon and stars above,
And suddenly, I'm reminded -
    There's no limit to God's love.

Each day He gives us sunlight
    So mortal eyes might see
The beauty of the heavens
    Reflected from each tree.

From honeybees in the clover,
    To the melody of birds,
Each creature is a testament
    Beyond our spoken words.

From the lilies of springtime,
    To summer's yellow rose,
God lets us know He loves us
    Through every flower that grows.

The seasons are reminders
    Controlled by Him above
To reassure us daily...
    There's no limit to God's love!

Clay Harrison

The Cozy Days

When Autumn's last faint crickets
Pass fleetingly away,
When frost is burned upon the urn
A new and crisp cold day.
When big plump cheeks are rosy
And cold weather is askew,
The winter chills upon the wills
Of folks like me and you.
It is the time of cozy weather
Of winter day by day,
When cloak, and quilt, and shawl,
and hearth
Help one to get away.
The winds at frosted windows
Replay their symphony,
Chill the edge of sill and ledge
Except where fire be.
We'll hide behind the walls of home
Enjoined in winter's thing,
Counting all of the cozy days
That take us back to spring.

James Joseph Huesgen

There's No Need to Worry

Through the darkness of this life,
I travel everyday;
but there's no need to worry,
for I have found "The Way."
And I know He will guide me,
wherever I must go,
so there's no need to worry,
God's word has told me so.
And there's no need to worry,
even in the darkest night,
for I'll keep looking forward,
and I will see His light.
And He will lead me down the road,
as narrow as it is,
but still no need to worry,
because the road is His.
So why waste any time at all,
not a minute, hour, or day,
when there's no need to worry,
once you have found "The Way."

George A. Hellard Jr.

Weather

I love to see the snow flakes fall
And cover everything in sight,
I feel an inner sense of peace
And safety when the world is white.
It seems I'm in a special spot
Wrapped in a blanket, soft and warm,
So nothing from outside this place
Can enter in and bring me harm.

When rain and wind both come at once
And thunder rolls across the sky,
The lightning's boney, burning hand
Pokes jagged fingers in my eye.
My very soul is now content
I'm free of all my fears and woe,
A thunderstorm can cleanse my heart,
I am enraptured with the snow.

Lavonne Childers Minigh

Winter Magic

What spirits haunt these silent woods,
With snow piled deep?
This vaulted sky of grey whose flakes
Fall while I sleep?
These marble hills and crystal lakes,
And frozen springs?
Of what forgotten time and place,
This forest sings!

The hills and hollows beckon me,
As hearthfires glow,
Outside my frosty windowpane,
A castle in the snow.
Tall trees stand like silver knights,
To lead the way,
Into a fairy kingdom, on
This winter day.

A drawbridge made of fallen limbs,
Spans silver moat,
Of narrow stream, beyond whose banks,
The magic wrought,
In vanished past awaits to claim
The hearts of those
Who enter here, as north winds sigh,
. . . Who goes? . . . Who goes? . . .

Grace E. Easley

23

Church Bells

The sound of church bells
Fill the air
They're here; they're there
They're everywhere,
They call us in to prayer.

Church bells ring
And church bells peal,
They make us sing
They make us feel
His presence everywhere.

Church bells ringing
Out at dawn,
Church bells
In the early morn,
Let's revel in their sound.

May church bells help us
Start the day
With happy thoughts,
Oh Lord we pray,
As we all gather round.

Marilyn McNeil de Latour

So Many Blessings

My blessings are so many
I cannot add them up,
God showers them down upon me
And daily fills my cup.

As gentle rain from heaven
Descends upon the ground,
So His love and mercy
Everywhere are found.

So when I feel like grumbling
I just pause a while
And start to count my blessings,
And then I have to smile.

Recalling all God's goodness
Dispels my gloom and woes,
My heart wells up with praises
And my cup overflows.

Rosemary J. Tivey

My cup runneth over.
Ps. 23:5

Snowfall

In the silence of the moonlight
Snowflakes tumble to the ground,
Weaving winterland enchantment
As they fall without a sound.

Snowflakes, tiny, pristine petals
Knitting coverlets of white,
Magically transforming hillsides
Into scenes of sheer delight.

In the quiet of the moment
With this frosty, tranquil view
Of a world now hushed by snowfall,
God, I feel so close to You.

As I gaze out from my window,
Hear, oh Lord, my whispered prayer,
Thanking You for all this beauty,
I find Your Love and goodness everywhere.

Polly Thornton

Today

Today - I must delay my labors
And the chores I do each day
To commune with God and Jesus
For Their gifts of yesterday.
I must take the time to worship
And to thank Them for Their Grace
That has kept me safe from evil
And endeared me, in embrace.

Just a little time together -
In the bonds of whispered prayer -
That will tell Them how I love Them
For Their guidance and Their care;
I must also ask Their blessings
On the paths I walk today -
Like the ones They graced upon me
And my paths of yesterday.

Michael Dubina

*May my words
and my thoughts
be acceptable to you,
O Lord, my rock
and redeemer.*
Ps. 19:14

The Art of Winter

Looking through the window
Into the sunny day,
I see the touch of winter
In all its great array.
Deserted nests in tree tops
Are topt with snowy lids,
And a frosty snowman's standing
In a sea of snow-white drifts.

White clouds that match the snowfall
Are blown by gusty winds,
And tiny snowflakes find a roost
On trees with leafless limbs.
Looking through the window
Into this sun-filled day,
I see the art of winter
Majestically displayed.

Loise Pinkerton Fritz